Commercial Real Estate Investing

The Ultimate Beginner's guide to learn how to invest in Commercial Real Estate and Build your Real Estate Empire.

Table of Contents

Why Commercial Real Estate and Who Commercial Real Estate is For

What Is Commercial Real Estate?

- Examples of Commercial Real Estate

- The Differences Between Commercial and Residential Real Estate

Reasons to Invest in Commercial Real Estate

- The Duration of a Lease

- Lease Assignment

- Commercial Tenants Pay Property Taxes

- Your Tenants Make Money On Your Premises

- Certainty of Getting Rent

- Upward-Only Rents

- Less Government Regulations

Potential Issues With Investing In Commercial Real Estate

- Much more difficult to find and get tenants

- Banks Will Not Cover The Entire Purchase Price of a Commercial Property

The Value of Real Estate

How to Find Tenants For Commercial Real Estate

How to Find Great Deals on Commercial Real Estate

- Ads in Newspapers

- Commercial Real Estate Brokers

- The Internet

- Being Attentive Every Day

- Word of Mouth Advertising

How to Analyze Deals

Conclusion

Free Bonus

Introduction: Why Commercial Real Estate and Who Commercial Real Estate is For.

Real estate has been in existence since people have decided that living in caves was no longer an option. However, most progress in real estate has probably happened in the last two century or so with the invention of the elevator. Elevators made it possible for real estate to include high-rise office buildings, multiple-floor residential apartment houses, and shopping malls.

Investing in commercial real estate is very different from dealing with residential properties. Oftentimes commercial real estate deals require very little or even no capital. While commercial estate can be very risky, it can also be very safe because of a number of things you can do with commercial buildings that you can't do with residential dwellings. We will discuss all these differences and strategies later on in this book.

Most people think that investing in commercial real estate is very similar to dealing with residential properties with the only differences being that that the money amounts are larger and contracts are longer. The reality is completely different.

There are a lot of distinctions between commercial and residential real estate when it comes to legal, practical and operational aspects.

Investing in commercial real estate is a great way to build wealth. The reason why commercial estate is a great vehicle for generating wealth can be explained in one word. This word is leverage. Leverage when applied to commercial real estate means that your returns from your commercial real estate investments can be much bigger than the time and effort you put into this business. Commercial properties are usually much more valuable than residential real estate such as apartments, condos or houses. This means that once you are able to apply strategies that we discuss later in this book, you will be able to acquire properties with very little money and witness the magical powers of leverage work wonders for you.

To invest in commercial real estate, you do not need a special license. If you are a principal in a commercial real estate transaction, you do not have to be licensed. A principal is someone who is participating in a transaction to make a profit. Agents and brokers help principals and get commissions for their work.

There are two advantages to obtaining a real estate license. The first one is that you will have access to the multiple listing service or MLS. The MLS is a suite of tools that allow real estate brokers access an extensive database of properties and information about them, and help cooperate with other brokers. The second advantage of holding a real estate license is that you will be able to get commissions when buying and selling properties that belong to you.

The disadvantage of holding a license is that you and your deals will become a subject of scrutiny by the authorities, especially if some of your deals do not work out. As a licensed person you are held to a much larger list of requirements compared to someone who does not hold a license.

There are many strategies when it comes to investing in commercial real estate, but at the end of the day your success depends on not whether you know a strategy, but how you implement it.

One thing you need to understand is that no matter the venture, there will always be people who will try to convince you that now is not the right time, that you can't do X because of the economy, climate, political reasons and so on. The bigger the project and the bigger the outcome, the more negativity you will get. This is why there are so many people who are convinced that it is impossible to make money by investing in commercial properties.

However, as an individual you and only you decide what you are going to do. You always have a choice and responsibility for your own actions. You can either listen to those who say that you can't do something or you can follow those who succeed and learn from them.

If you believe that to invest in commercial real estate you need to have a lot of money and that dealing with commercial real estate is incredibly difficult, then these beliefs will find a way to manifest themselves in your life. If, however, you have an open mind and are willing to learn about simple and interesting new opportunities, then this book is definitely for you.

© **Copyright 2016 by Mark Thomas - All rights reserved.**

This document is geared towards providing exact and reliable information in regards to the topic and issue covered. The publication is sold with the idea that the publisher is not required to render accounting, officially permitted, or otherwise, qualified services. If advice is necessary, legal or professional, a practiced individual in the profession should be ordered.

- From a Declaration of Principles which was accepted and approved equally by a Committee of the American Bar Association and a Committee of Publishers and Associations.

In no way is it legal to reproduce, duplicate, or transmit any part of this document in either electronic means or in printed format. Recording of this publication is strictly prohibited and any storage of this document is not allowed unless with written permission from the publisher. All rights reserved.

The information provided herein is stated to be truthful and consistent, in that any liability, in terms of inattention or otherwise, by any usage or abuse of any policies, processes, or directions contained within is the solitary and utter responsibility of the recipient reader. Under no circumstances will any legal responsibility or blame be held against the publisher for any reparation, damages, or monetary loss due to the information herein, either directly or indirectly.

Respective authors own all copyrights not held by the publisher.

The information herein is offered for informational purposes solely, and is universal as so. The presentation of the information is without contract or any type of guarantee assurance.

The trademarks that are used are without any consent, and the publication of the trademark is without permission or backing by the trademark owner. All trademarks and brands within this book are for clarifying purposes only and are the owned by the owners themselves, not affiliated with this document.

What Is Commercial Real Estate?

Before we get to discussing commercial real estate strategies, deals and finding tenants, we need to define what commercial real estate is and what it is not.

You may be absolutely confident that a three-bedroom, two bathroom home is residential real estate and a block that consists of five retail stores is commercial real estate, but what about a set of seven units in an apartment complex that both brokers and banks consider to be commercial real estate? Truth of the matter is, banks and insurance companies often classify buildings with four or more units as commercial real estate even when the buildings themselves consist of residential dwellings.

However, for the purposes of this book, we will use the following approach: real estate where people live is residential and real estate where businesses conduct commercial activities is commercial.

This concept allows up to easily classify any piece of real estate. For example, houses, apartments, condominiums are all residential real estate while retail stores, offices, plants and factories, hotels, airports, and hospitals are commercial real estate.

You may be wondering if we are contradicting our own definition by calling hotels commercial real estate. If you do, notice the following difference: if you lease your building to a hotel, you are leasing it to someone who will use it to conduct commercial activities in it. The same principle applies to doctors renting out a part of a private home. They are not living there and they are using the space to conduct commercial activities. Therefore, the real estate is considered to be commercial.

Here are some examples of commercial real estate:

Offices

Warehouses

Retail Stores, Centers, and Shopping Malls

Hotels and motels

Resort properties

Land developments

Amusement parks

Hospitals

Doctor's offices

Paint shops

Warehouses

Airports

Let's now make a detailed comparison of the differences between commercial and residential real estate, so that you can see for yourself how they are different.

In short, this difference can be described in the following way: with residential real estate you are really dealing with people when with commercial real estate you are really dealing with agreements and contracts.

It is true that to rent out commercial properties you need to find tenants and negotiate with them, which means dealing with people. It is also true that residential real estate also has a significant number of paperwork including application forms, background checks, lease agreements and so on.

This being said, with residential dwellings, you or your property managers will be getting calls about toilets not working, faucets leaking and so on. You may get a letter from a local community board telling that that the grass on your property is too long or that the fence is too high. While you can hire property managers to deal with the majority of these issues, investing and renting residential real estate is still a business that is focused around dealing with people.

Things are very different in commercial real estate. A lease document is a central document. It may be several pages long and usually describes even minor details of your relationship with your tenants. Most likely you will never get a phone call about a leaking faucet because most commercial leases say that it's the responsibility of a tenant to keep the property in a fully functioning condition. This is why absolute majority of commercial tenants are aware of the fact that they will have to deal with all the maintenance and repair issues such as cleaning the carpets, replacing broken locks and fixing toilets and leaking faucets. In most cases, the landlord of a commercial property is only responsible for the roofs and walls. Even painting the exterior and maintaining the property grounds are the responsibilities of your tenants.

With residential real estate, your options when your tenants are late with paying rent may be severely limited. For example, in California, a residential property landlord can't take any significant steps until the rent is late ninety days or more.

With commercial real estate, depending on jurisdiction, you may have the right to enter the premises and seize all the property as little as after two weeks after the rent due date.

Reasons to Invest in Commercial Real Estate

In this chapter, we will discuss the reasons why you would want to invest in commercial properties. These reasons are also what makes commercial real estate different from residential properties.

The Duration of a Lease

A residential tenancy is often annual. Sometimes it may last for just six months or even be month-to-month. Two-year leases are possible but are somewhat rare. Commercial leases are usually much longer in duration. Month-to-month leases usually only occur at the end of a very long lease when the two parties have not made any definite decisions about their next steps. A typical commercial lease may last for two, three, five or ten years. In big cities like New York tenants prefer really long leases to make sure that they can stay in a neighborhood even if the prices start going up. In London, United Kingdom, leases with twenty-five year durations were typical until very recently. Leases that last for ten, fifteen and twenty years are typical when you are dealing with banks or large retailers. The reason for it is simple: big retailer most likely needs the premises to look a certain way, which means that the company will need to invest a lot of money into your space. It doesn't make financial sense to re-do a property with a short lease.

All of this means that with commercial real estate you will have to deal with fewer lease renewals compared to residential real estate. If you have a big bank as a tenant with even years remaining on a fifteen-year lease, you know that for the next ten years you will have a steady flow of income. While there are risks in any business, renting a space to a company with a long history and solid financials can give you an incredible sense of certainty in your future. In can also allow you to budget your finances for a longer period of time, calculate your income streams and expand your business with security and confidence.

Having tenants who conduct commercial activities on your property is very different from dealing with residential tenants. Your commercial tenants most likely spend a lot of money advertising their location. They also spend a lot on various marketing materials and promotions that mention the address. If your tenants had to move, they would most likely lose a lot of their current clients. This makes commercial tenants really interested in longer leases. As a commercial real estate investor, you will have your tenants contact you in the middle of a ten-year or even longer lease asking you to extend or renew the lease.

There are two reasons for your tenants to do so. First, they may be considering a major renovation of their facility, and such a renovation may only make sense if they were to stay at the location for a long period of time.

The second reason is when your tenant is thinking about selling their business. In this case, the fact that the new owner of the business will have a guaranteed lease allows them to sell the business at a higher price. For example, if a business has only a year remaining on their lease, a new owner may be very reluctant about buying it and losing a lot of customers due to a change in location.

Hopefully, you can now see how longer leases in commercial real estate work to the benefit of both the owner and the tenant of a property.

Lease Assignment

In addition to being able to enter the property and seize the belongings of a non-paying tenant most commercial properly leases come with an assignment of lease clause.

If a residential tenant decides to move out in the middle of his or her lease, he or she is still responsible for the rent until the expiration of the lease. However, if he or she finds a new tenant, most landlords will accept the switch. If the new tenant is unable to pay the rent, your only option is to deal with the new tenant. The old tenant is not responsible for anything after he or she moves out from the dwelling.

With commercial property leases, you actually can go to the original tenant to collect the rent even in the case of a lease substitute. When a tenant sells the business or finds a substitute, there is usually an assignment of a lease between the three parties: the landlord, the old tenant and the new tenant. This assignment of lease holds the old tenant liable in case the new tenant is in default of their responsibilities under the original lease.

Things like these happen with commercial properties because a commercial lease is considered to be a very serious commitment from all the involved parties. The bankruptcy of a tenant is one of the rare exceptions when a tenant can get out of a commercial lease. Otherwise, a tenant could get out of a lease by selling their business to someone for one dollar and walking away from their commitment. The way commercial leases are set, sellers of businesses know that they effectively assume responsibility for the buyer of the business until the lease expires. This makes business buyers more confident and guarantees that sellers are interested in the success of the business under the new management.

Commercial Tenants Pay Property Expenses

With residential properties, it is common for tenants to pay only the rent. The landlords do not expect their tenants to pay real estate taxes, insurance premiums or cover maintenance. This is why net returns from residential real estate investments are usually much lower than the gross returns. When investing in residential real estate, you have the responsibility for taxes, insurance, maintenance and legal compliance.

This is not how things work with commercial leases. It is common for tenants to cover rent, property taxes, maintenance, and insurance. This happens because the tenants usually refurbish the space according to their standards and requirements. Once they do so, it is easier for everyone when the tenants deal with insurance, compliance, and tax responsibilities directly. Commercial leases that include base rent, taxes, insurance, and maintenance are also known in the real estate industry as triple leases. Triple leases are different from regular leases in that your net returns on such leases are equal to your gross returns.

You could also add all the expenses into the base rent, but it is not a good idea. There is always a chance that your municipality will increase the real estate tax on your property. Your insurance rates may also go up for different reasons, especially during a very long lease. If you bundle up all the expenses into one price, tax and insurance increases may look to your tenants as an increase in rent. You do not want this to happen, which is why separation of the base rent and the additional costs is a smart way to go.

Your Tenants Make Money On Your Premises

While this fact may sound obvious, it does lead to two non-obvious effects.

First, when something on the property breaks, your tenants would be interested in fixing it as quickly as possible. Residential tenants are usually willing to wait for a few days for a repairman to show up because this way they are saving money. Commercial tenants lose money when they wait. This is why they want everything fixed as quickly as possible. They are operating a business and not being able to conduct business means losing money. Business people are usually entrepreneurs, meaning that they have a go-getting "let's fix this as quickly as possible" spirit and are not interested in waiting for someone so that they can save a little bit of money.

This attitude is very different from the attitude

of residential tenants, who often see themselves as victims whose rent is going into paying the mortgage of the landlord and who are trying to get every penny they can from the landlord, even if it means having to wait and experience a lot of inconveniences. Obviously, not all residential tenants are like this, but the general rule stands. Residential tenants expect their landlords to pay for things while commercial tenants are much more likely to fix the issues themselves.

The second unobvious consequence from the fact that your commercial tenants are making money on your property is that your tenants are directly interested in your property being in the best possible condition. A residential tenant may view his or her apartment as a place where they come to get some rest from work and that's it. They may have zero interest in keeping your property in good shape and there's nothing you can do about it. They also may be saving money to buy their own property and treat yours as a temporary solution that is not worth the effort of keeping it in shape. This is not the case with commercial tenants, especially with tenants in retail properties where in order to be attractive to the customers the entire store may need an expensive quality renovation every few years or so. Under the terms of most commercial leases such renovations require permission from the landlord, but they don't require any of your

investments, which means that you are getting the best of both worlds. You are getting your property renovated and you are not paying a dime for it.

Certainty of Getting Rent

Residential tenants almost always sign a rental lease in their name. They also pay the rent personally. Typically, they do it in one of the three following forms: cash, check or money order.

When your tenants pay rent in cash someone needs to pick it up. While you don't have to do it yourself and can delegate it to your property manager, a lot of things can go wrong. Your car can get a flat tire when you are driving. Your tenant can be late to the bank or lose his or her job and not have the funds available.

The same scenario applies when you are getting paid by check or money order. You either need to pick up the check or money order in person or your tenant mails it to you. If they do mail it to you, the envelope needs to be addressed properly and have the right amount of postage, the check needs to have no typos and so on. In all these scenarios a lot of things can go wrong.

Commercial tenants are very different from residential tenants. First, the lease is usually in the name of the company. The rent is one of the fixed expenses that they need to pay on time to avoid potential issues and breaks in making money, which makes paying it on time a priority matter.

Most often your commercial tenants are very

busy, so they want to avoid paying in cash or by check and having to meet you. Most commercial tenants pay their rent by automatic bank transfer. It is easier and more convenient both for them and for you.

With residential tenants, a sequence of events needs to happen in order for you to get your rent. The tenant needs to go to the bank or write out a check, then give it to you or mail it to you and so on. If something goes wrong during one or more of the steps, you are not getting paid on time. In contrast, with commercial tenants, you get your payment by default. An action is needed for you not to get paid, such as contacting the bank to stop the payment. This means that with commercial real estate it doesn't really matter where you are located geographically or where your tenant is located. It also doesn't matter if you or your tenant is busy or vacationing. If everything has been setup, you are getting paid.

Upward-Only Rents

With leases of six months to one-year residential real estate and the price that you can charge for your rentals depend significantly on the short-term market conditions. The rent you charge for a residential dwelling may go up or it may go down similarly to the prices of gas, stock, and coffee.

Residential rental prices tend to go down when the overall market goes down. However, this doesn't usually happen with commercial real estate. Most commercial real estate leases have an "upward-only" clause included. This means that the rent can't go down. It can stay the same or it can go up. While this clause may seem unfair to the tenants, in reality, it provides stability to the rental market of commercial real estate. If the clause wasn't there, commercial real estate owners would need to build a buffer into their rent prices. They would need some kind of protection for the scenarios when the rent is going down. Upward-only clauses serve as a protection and ensure that commercial real estate market does not fluctuate too much, which would not be in the interest of both tenants and landlords.

Less Government Regulations

Most countries and municipalities have very strict laws when it comes to the relationship between residential tenants and their landlords. Some of these laws are very reasonable, such as the ones that require landlords to give tenants notices before property inspections. Others, however, are completely unfair to the landlords, such as, for example, a California law that prevents landlords from taking any action for ninety days after a tenant stops paying rent.

Commercial real estate and relationships between commercial tenants and landlords have much fewer government regulations. If a commercial tenant stops paying rent, the landlord can take steps very quickly. These steps are similar to what a bank can do with someone who stops paying their car loan.

Potential Issues With Investing In Commercial Real Estate

While investing in commercial real estate has a lot of advantages that we have discussed in the previous chapter, it also has potential issues.

Much more difficult to find and get tenants

If you have a residential rental property that has been on the market for thirty or more days and you can't find a renter, there is only one reason, which is also a solution that you can implement very quickly. The color of the carpet, the color of the walls, outdated kitchen or old bathrooms are not the reasons why the property is still on the market. The only reason why you don't have a tenant is because the market thinks that the price of your rental is too high. Lower the price and you will get a tenant very quickly.

Unfortunately, this is not how things work in commercial real estate. The fact that you don't have tenants may have very little to do with the price of your commercial rental. Most commercial properties are only suitable for a very narrow list of activities. A bank is not going to be interested in a retail store space and vice versa. You can't fit a commercial operation into a property just because you want to or just because someone would like to be there because the price is within their budget. There is no way that a factory would be of interest to a clothing retailer looking for a space in a location with a lot of foot traffic. This is why it can quite difficult to find a tenant for a commercial property. This is one of the main reasons why new investors tend to stay away from the commercial real estate. Commercial properties can sometimes stay empty for months or even years.

Banks Will Not Cover The Entire Purchase Price of a Commercial Property

Banks are usually willing to help residential real estate investors cover a significant percentage of the purchase price. Banks will often lend residential real estate investors up to eighty percent of the price of the residential real estate without requiring them to purchase mortgage insurance. If you are a residential real estate investor willing to buy mortgage insurance, you may even find a bank that will lend you ninety, ninety-five or even one hundred percent of the real estate value.

Banks are much less willing to tolerate risks with commercial real estate. You can usually get up to fifty or sixty percent loan. This results in the perception that you need a lot of money to become a commercial real estate investor.

However, this is not always the case. To understand why you first need to understand the value of real estate and what buyers and sellers are looking for. This is what we will discuss in the next chapter.

The Value of Real Estate

There are a lot of factors that determine that value of residential real estate. These factors include the size of the property, the age of the construction, number of bedrooms and bathrooms, quality and age of fixtures, presence of amenities, the possibility of flooding, hurricanes and other natural disasters, proximity to schools, shopping and restaurants, crime and school statistics and more.

However, a three-bedroom two-bathroom home that is twenty years old and is in great condition will sell for almost the same price as a similar three-bedroom two-bathroom home in a neighborhood nearby. This is also true of apartments in the big cities. An apartment of the same square footage will sell for almost the same price as a similar apartment in the same neighborhood.

Furthermore, the value of a residential property almost never depends on whether it has tenants with a lease or not. If anything, having tenants in a residential dwelling may reduce its value by making it really unattractive to people who are looking to move in quickly.

The return an investor can get from a residential property depends on two factors: the rental income and the purchase price. Both or these factors can fluctuate and depend only on the market. There is very little an investor can do.

The value of a commercial property depends on the rental income and the capitalization rate. The capitalization rate is the rate at which rental income achieves capital value. For example, if a property costs $100,000 and generates 10,000 in return every year, its capitalization rate or cap rate is 10%.
The market determines capitalization rates. If

the market cap rate is 12% and you find a building for sale that will bring you 8% a year, all other factors being equal, this is not a good deal.

If the rate is 10% and you find a building that will bring you 15%, then this is a terrific investment.

Obviously, cap rates are different in different parts of the country. For example, there is always demand for commercial real estate on Wall Street in New York City, because investors know that they will always be able to find tenants who want to have an office with a Wall Street address. This is why historically capitalization rates on Wall Street have been around five percent, meaning that you would have to pay around $2 million for a property that would generate $100,000 of rental income in a year.

In a smaller town capitalization rates can be as high at 25%, meaning that you will need to spend $400,000 to get a property that will bring you $100,000 in rental income annually.

Why is there such a difference? The difference exists because it is a reward for the skill, experience and tenacity in finding new tenants for commercial real estate. It is easy to find occupants for an office on Wall Street and so the cap rate is low. It is much harder to do it in a smaller town, which results in much higher capitalization rates.

This means that if you know how to find tenants for commercial real estate, you can make a lot of money where others can't. You can also make deals that do not require a lot of capital. This is something that is simply not possible with residential real estate. We will discuss finding commercial tenants in the next chapter.

How to Find Tenants For Commercial Real Estate

Today we live is a very self-centered society. The most important word in marketing is the word "you." Your marketing and advertising need to be focused on "you", meaning your customers. All your efforts need to convey to your prospects the benefits and features of what they will get when they sign a lease with you. A lot of real estate investors get into business and focus on themselves without realizing that they can get anything they want if they help their customers get what they want.

How to rent out a funeral home

Let's now take a look at a case that you will most likely find in many of the smaller towns all across North America. Suppose you come across a funeral parlor in a small town that has been sitting on the market for four years. It is not hard to guess what is happening. The property probably has a very specific layout, so not too many businesses are interested in leasing it. There also probably isn't anyone in

the town opening a new funeral parlor. Also, most likely it is probably very hard for people to imagine owning or redesigning a funeral home unless they are already in the funeral business. However, at the same time funeral industry is not shrinking and definitely has room for growth.

When a property stays on the market for some time, it usually "goes stale." This applies to both residential and commercial properties. Investors look at the time that the property has been on the market and do not want to buy it because they assume that there is something wrong with it since no one purchased it during a long period of time.

The first thing you want to find out if you stumble across a property like this is where and how often it has been advertised. You will often find that the listing agent only advertised a few times in a local newspaper. Many listing agents take too many listings and do not have enough resources to pay attention to them all. Some agents are flat out negligent and lazy. They put a few ads with bad pictures and terrible descriptions and then blame the property for not selling. If you find a scenario like this, it means that there's definitely some opportunity there.

Now let's also assume that the property has been listed at a local auction, but did not sell because the bids did not exceed the reserve price of $175,000.

What conclusions can you make so far? You will probably make two of them. The first one is that there is no high demand for funeral parlors. The second one is that the owner is not willing to sell the funeral home for anything less than $175,000.

Truth is, both of these conclusions are absolutely wrong. You can't decide that there is no demand for funeral homes because the listing agent did a terrible job of advertising the property. He only did so locally, and even locally he didn't do it well. Secondly, while the owner may have had the price of $175,000 in mind at the time of the auction, with the property being on the market for three years he or she probably has different expectations in the present moment and the actual price is much lower.

So, what can you do in this scenario? You can find an assistant for $10-$15/hr in the United States or $3-$5/hr in the Philippines to call funeral homes in the neighboring cities. You can ask them if they would be interested in expanding to the town where the $175,000 funeral home for sale is located.

When cold-calling this way, you would definitely have some people hang up on you. Some will be amused. Some will tell you that you are crazy. However, there is a significant chance that you will find someone who will be interested. In any case, even at $10-$15/hr, this will not cost you much.

Next, you could tell the interested party that you had a building for sale and could get them all the details if they were interested. Here's why you would say that the building was for sale: the last thing you want is a lease with a person who things that you only got them as a tenant because you were the first to buy the property. If the person refuses, you can offer them to become their landlord. You can then show the property and sign an agreement that constitutes a lease contingent on you buying the property.

Notice that at this point you have not bought the property neither did you spend any significant amount of money. Now, if your annual rent for the building is $30,000, at 12% capitalization rate this would mean that the building is worth $250,000. At the same time, you know that the owner is willing to sell it for $175,000 or less. You also have a lease agreement contingent on you buying the building. At this point, all you have to do is find a lender who would support you in finishing the operation.

How to Fill A Warehouse

Another segment of commercial real estate that most people believe is hard to rent out is a warehouse. Here's what you could try: obtain a list of all warehouses in your area. Then hire someone to cold-call the tenants and ask them if they need more space or if they need to downsize when their lease is up. Just like in the first example you won't spend a lot of money and yet have a pretty good chance of making a deal.

How to find tenants using real estate brokers

Real estate brokers can be a great source of leads for commercial real estate investors. They usually have lists of prospective tenants looking for very specific properties. This list can be sorted by the geographic area, the type of property, square footage and so on.

One disadvantage of dealing with real estate brokers is that they would usually want a commission and in commercial real estate this commission is for the entire duration of a lease. However, this amount does vary from region to region and from city to city, so be sure to find out the customs and traditions of the real estate industry in your area.

In any case, make sure you understand exactly what the financial structure is before you start working with commercial real estate agents. Also find out if your real estate agent will get a fee if you rent your property on your own. Some companies force their clients into signing exclusive agreements. An agreement like that means that while you have a contract with your broker, your broker gets paid no matter who brought the tenant in. So if you are under a bad contract, you may have an obligation to pay a fee even if your broker didn't do anything and you ended up finding a tenant through your own connections.

Splitting a large tenancy into multiple smaller tenancies

Sometimes it makes sense to break a large vacant property into a number of smaller tenancies. For example, there may be a 20,000-square-foot property available, but not a lot of demand for such properties. You may have a difficulty finding a tenant at $30 per square foot. However, if you break up the property into four units of 5,000 square feet each, you may be able to find tenants at $40 per square foot.

Keep in mind that dividing a property into multiple tenancies may be complicated and expensive. The dividing wall will most likely need soundproofing and fireproofing. You will need to install additional meters for electricity and gas and you will need four main entrances instead of just one. You will probably need new fire escapes, too. However, even if the changes cost $75,000, they may make sense depending on how much rent you can collect from your new tenants.

Consolidating multiple properties into one

Sometimes you may have a hard time finding a tenant for a big space. Sometimes in may work the other way around and you will not be able to find multiple tenants for multiple small spaces. In this case, it may make sense to consolidate multiple properties into one large tenancy.

The Best Way To Get a Tenant

As we have discussed earlier in this book, the value of commercial real estate equals to rental income from the property divided by the capitalization rate of the property. There is nothing you can do about the capitalization rate. It is the market that defines what the rate is going to be. At the same time, there are a lot of things you can do to increase the rental income from a property. If a piece of commercial real estate is sitting on the market empty, its value is going to be very low. If it has a tenant with a long lease who is willing to remodel the place, the value of the property may increase very significantly. In other words, rental income is something you can influence and something that has a direct impact on the value of your property. If you have a good tenant, you building is worth a lot of money. If you don't have a tenant, the price of your commercial real estate goes down.

Sometimes a commercial real estate owner may get into real trouble. This usually happens when the property is sitting empty, and the owner has to pay taxes, maintenance, and insurance from his or her pocket. These costs may even lead to bankruptcy.

Having a piece of property and no tenant is the worst scenario in commercial real estate. The best possible scenario, however, is not having a property and a tenant. It is having tenants, but no building.

Imagine owning a commercial building and advertising it. Eventually, you will start getting calls or emails and will rent out the building. At the same time, it is highly likely that the calls and emails are going to continue. You could simply say that you found a tenant, or you could do something else because you now have a number of people looking to rent a property from you. You could ask the callers about what they are looking for. Then you could try to go and find something suitable for them. This means that instead of finding properties and then looking for tenants it is much smarter and more profitable to find tenants first and then look for properties.

Why would someone deal with you instead of simply hiring a real estate agent? The answer is simple: with an agent, they will have to pay full market rent on a piece of real estate. If you find a great deal, you may give your tenants a break on the rent and still make a significant profit.

The more people you know and the more you are willing to talk to different people who rent commercial real estate, the more requests you will have.

How to Find Great Deals on Commercial Real Estate

One of the questions that commercial real estate beginners have is about finding great deals. The answer to the question "How do you find a great deal?" is always the same: there is no magic pill. You need to use a variety of methods.

Ads in Newspapers

Imagine someone who owns a commercial real estate building. Chances are, you are not thinking about someone who is twenty years old. Most likely, in your mind, you have a picture of an older person. The older someone is, the higher the chances that their life does not revolve exclusively around the Internet.

This is why you want to make sure that you pay attention to local newspapers and ads in them. You will find a lot of owners willing to sell their properties due to health issues, retirement, and family circumstances. Often properties that you will find in small ads are going to turn out much more lucrative than those that are advertised on popular websites or big banners. Big ads are usually placed by real estate agents or by people who want to attract a lot of attention to their property, which to you means a lot of competition.

People who place small ads are usually looking to avoid big marketing expenses and dealing with real estate agents and paying all the commissions. They want a quick deal and are looking for someone who will give them what they are looking for without any major hassles.

Commercial Real Estate Brokers

Commercial real estate brokers are yet another

great source of leads for finding deals on commercial real estate. Make sure that you are on the mailing lists of both large and small commercial real estate firms in your area. You also want to stay in touch with solo agents that work by themselves. Arrange a few meetings, inform them about what you are looking for and keep in touch to make sure that they remember about you and will inform you about properties should something interesting to you become available.

A lot of people tend to stay away from real estate agents because they want to avoid commissions. In most cases, it is the seller of a property who pays the commission. Brokers will have information about the people who have decided to use a broker. Therefore, you are not losing anything by dealing with a commercial real estate broker when looking to acquire a property.

A lot of commercial real estate investors also

choose to stay away from agents who are also commercial real estate investors themselves. Such investors think that the agent-investor is not going to show them any good deals and would keep all the best properties to himself or herself. In reality, there is a number of reasons why an investor-agent may choose to pass on a property. It may be that he or she does not have enough money. It also may be that he or she does not specialize in a certain kind of commercial real estate or doesn't have the right tenants for the property.

At the same time, an investor-agent is not going to lose your time talking to you about deals that make no sense. Your work with an investor-agent may result in a partnership that is beneficial to both sides.

The Internet

While we did start this chapter with discussing

newspaper ads and dealing with real estate agents, we are not dismissing the Internet or its power. The Internet can be a great resource for commercial real estate leads and deals. Today it is possible to find listings, communicate with tenants, sellers, buyers and agents, submit offers, conduct your research, apply for loans and insurance and even manage a property through the Internet. Obviously, the Internet is also making you location-free, which means that you can explore and invest in markets that are located in different parts of the country far away from each other.

Regularly visit the websites that have commercial real estate listings. Unfortunately, the problem with the Internet is that it is easy to find listings not only for you but also for your competition. However, even with this is it worthwhile to visit the websites often.

Being Attentive Every Day

A great source of leads is to always to be on the lookout for what is going on around you. You may notice a "For Rent" sign suddenly pop-up when a property owner is trying to see whether he or she can rent the property without going to a real estate agent. A sign that says "For Sale By Owner" is a surefire way to know that there is no real estate agent involved in the deal. Often you will also see signs that say that the building is for sale or lease. This means that the owner can't find a good tenant and is willing to settle for either selling or renting the building. Such signs mean that there is a definite opportunity for a great deal.

When driving or walking around you will also see buildings that do not have any signs, but sure look as the owner would appreciate any offer. Such buildings are usually in a really bad condition, have uncared lawns, a lot of trash and windows covered in dust. You can go to the county's assessor office or whatever it is called in your municipality, find who the owner is and contact them inquiring about buying the property.

It is also a great idea to take different routes when commuting to your office or picking and dropping kids from school. Do not stick to one road or one way to go. Take different routes at different times and pay attention to what is going on along the way.

Word of Mouth Advertising

While all the methods for attracting clients that we have discussed above do work and do so quite effectively, the best method is when the tenants seek you themselves because they have heard about you from their friends, acquaintances or connections. This is why you want as many people as possible to know that you are on the lookout for deals. Your aunt

Betty may not be interested in becoming a tenant in a commercial property. She may also not come up with ten people that you should talk to. However, in six months you may hear from aunt Betty's dentist who learned from her about the fact that you are in the commercial real estate business and who now wants to talk to you.

How can you accomplish that? First, you need to be talking to more people. Watching less mindless television and cutting the time that you spend on activities that do not bring you any pleasure and do not help you get closer to your goals is a great idea.

Next, take out your business card and look at it. Most likely you have your name in big letters and then, in small letters, something similar to "Vice President." The first thing you want to do is change your title to "Commercial Real Estate Investor." Even better, replace "Investor" with

"Deal Maker." The second thing you need to understand is that no one really cares about your name. This is why you want your name in a smaller font compared to "Commercial Real Estate Deal Maker." Finally, you may want to add a tagline to your business card, such as "I buy commercial buildings and help commercial tenants find perfect spaces for them."

How to Analyze Deals

If you think about the funeral parlor deal that we discussed earlier, you will see that there's really not much to analyze. You have a great opportunity. You see the building and its condition. The owner of the property has been around for years and has a great reputation.

However, not all commercial deals are this straightforward. A commercial property may have a number of titles, plot ratios, leasable premises and tenants on a number of leases.

This is the case where you would want to perform due diligence on a property. Due diligence means finding enough information about a property to be confident that the property is a good deal. It includes a review of financial records, property titles and anything else relevant to the property.

The first step of a due diligence process should be to verify that the seller is the actual legal owner of the property. The sellers can and often do perform due diligence on the buyers. The main thing they are interested in is the buyer's ability to purchase the property.

There are two types of due diligence that you want to perform. The first one consists of items that are hard to describe in numbers such as street appeal, good highway access, how close the property is to an airport, or how much foot traffic the property gets. This last piece of information is an example of a number that you can find out, but it's hard to decide what to do with it.

Fortunately, most of these items will be reflected in the market trends for the area. Properties with great transportation options and high volumes of foot traffic usually rent and sell for a higher amount compared to properties that don't have great features.

While there is not a formula to include all these factors into the equation, you need to become aware of the trends in your area in order to be able to make intelligent decisions about various commercial properties.

The second part of due diligence consists of hard facts such as the total land area, total square footage of the building, taxes, insurance and so on. In this part of due diligence, you want to verify all the numbers and make sure that they are correct.

Conclusion

Most people would agree that real estate industry is extremely large. Few, however, realize how large it really is or take any steps to learn more about it or enter it.
I want to congratulate you for taking the first step and reading this book.

Almost everyone lives in a house or an apartment. Every store that we go to, every school that our kids go to, are all real estate. The industry is extremely large and so are the opportunities.

In this book we talked about the benefits of real estate, finding deals, analyzing deals and doing due diligence.

One of the things to remember is that you need to be patient. The first building you look at most likely will not turn into a deal. Generally, the rule 100 to 10 to 3 to 1 would apply to your deals. This means that you will have to look at 100 properties and there will be 10 that you will be interested in. Out of 10 offers, 3 will get accepted and 1 will go through.

In other words, finding a great commercial property is also a numbers game. The good news is that the longer you are in the game, the more experience and connections you will have and the better deals you'll make.

We sincerely want to wish you a lot of luck and success on this journey!

Thank you again for downloading this book!

If you enjoyed this book, then I'd like to ask you for a favor, would you be kind enough to leave a review for this book on Amazon? It'd be greatly appreciated!

Thank you and good luck! ☺

-Mark Thomas

www.ingramcontent.com/pod-product-compliance
Lightning Source LLC
Chambersburg PA
CBHW070522210526
45169CB00027B/968